DESIGNS FOR

BEADED JEWELLERY

USING GLASS BEADS

DESIGNS FOR

BEADED JEWELLERY

USING GLASS BEADS

MARIA DI SPIRITO

SEARCH PRESS

First published in Great Britain 2006 by Search Press Limited,
Wellwood, North Farm Road, Tunbridge Wells, Kent TN2 3DR

Originally published in Italy 2005 by Il Castello Collane Tecniche, Milan

English translation by Karen Waloschek in association with
First Edition Translations Ltd, Cambridge

ISBN-10: 1-84448-164-6
ISBN-13: 978-1-84448-164-4

Photography by G. Cigolini

All the jewellery in this book was made from materials supplied by
FANTASY CRAFT of Milan, www.fantasycraft.it

Printed by Leo Paper Products Ltd, China

1 2 3 4   2005 2006 2007 2008

Contents

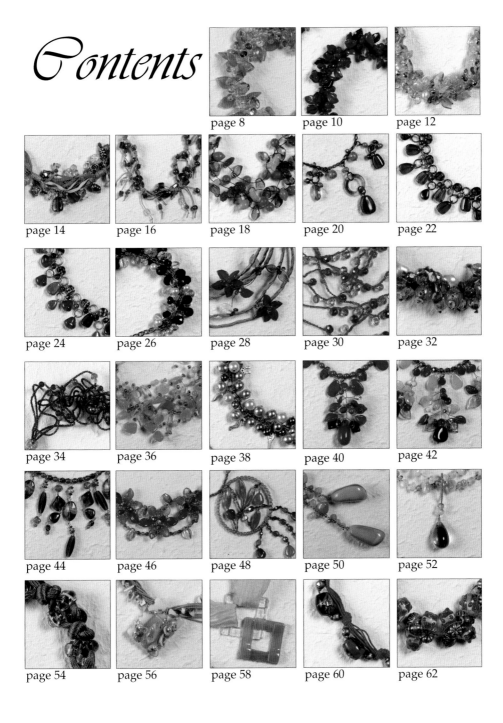

Introduction

Maria di Spirito presents her wonderful new beading collection.

Summery, colourful, young, classical, elegant, or romantic; whatever the style, every piece of jewellery has been made using nothing but glass beads. There are forty-eight original creations made with crystals, variously shaped, stamped Venetian or Czech glass beads and the latest yarns, chains and assembly components.

This book is dedicated to jewellery devotees. It is not a technical manual, but a collection of various styles of jewellery for different levels of jewellery-making ability. It offers the experienced jewellery-maker new ideas and suggestions for novel ways of combining materials and colours. On the other hand, those who are exploring jewellery making for the first time will be inspired to try this exciting new hobby.

With so many examples, jewellery lovers will not be able to resist creating something for themselves, as a present for someone special, or to sell. With patience and enthusiasm you will overcome any little difficulties and the beautiful results will make this a hugely rewarding hobby.

Maria di Spirito

Spring choker with pink glass leaves and flowers

Without cutting the metal wire from the spool, thread with a sequence of 4 beads alternating with decorations like leaves, flowers and differently coloured crystal trios. The 4 beads should be loose, and the decorations mounted on loops. Thread at least 20cm (8in) of beads and decorations and cut from the spool. Repeat until you have 6 strands 55cm (21½in) long. Plait the threads into a three-headed braid, making sure that all the decorative elements face the same side. Join together the wires in the bead tips and close with a spring clasp and chain.

Difficulty level: very complex

Designer: Maria di Spirito

Materials:

Metal wire
Bead tips
Pins and small rings
Spring clasp and chain
4mm pink glass beads
Pink glass leaves
Pink glass fantasy beads of various shades, shapes and sizes

Tools:

Wire cutters
Flat nose pliers
Round nose pliers
Scissors

Autumn choker with red leaves and crystal beads

Make up 4 threads following the instructions for the Spring choker with pink glass leaves and flowers (see page 8). This time, alternate 3 crystal beads (4mm) with loop-mounted beads made up of alternating leaves, flowers and crystal trios. When the 4 threads are ready, plait them into a braid, making sure that all the decorations face the same side. Join together the wires in the bead tips and close with a spring clasp and chain.

Difficulty level: very complex

Designer: Maria di Spirito

Materials:

Bead tips
Pins and small rings
Spring clasp and chain
0.4mm black copper wire
Red 4mm and 6mm rose-cut crystal beads
0.4mm and 0.6mm red glass beads
Red and anthracite glass leaves

Tools:

Wire cutters
Flat nose pliers
Round nose pliers

Summer choker with blue leaves and flowers

Follow the instructions for the Spring choker with pink glass leaves and flowers (see page 8). This time alternate 3 crystal beads with loops mounted with an alternating sequence of leaves, flowers and crystal trios.

Difficulty level: very complex

Materials:

Clamshell bead tips
Pins and small rings
Spring clasp and chain
0.4mm silver thread
4mm two-tone blue crystal beads
Glass leaves in blue, opal and wisteria
Beads of various shades and sizes

Tools:

Wire cutters
Flat nose pliers
Round nose pliers
Scissors

13

Pink faux suede choker

Insert a pin through each of the beads and metal spacers, bend each pin tip to form a loop and attach to a larger ring. Tie together 7 faux suede ribbons using spiral knots in coloured waxed cord. Hang the glass beads and metal spacers from the ribbons. Glue the ribbons into the bead tips. Close with a spring clasp.

Difficulty level: complex

Designer: Maria di Spirito

Materials:

4mm pink and ivory
faux suede ribbons
1mm pink waxed cord
Silver-plated headpins
and rings
0.3mm silver wire
Glass beads of various styles
and colours
Bead tips
Spring clasp and chain

Tools:

Flat nose pliers
Round nose pliers
Scissors

Pink necklaces

For the cord and pink bead necklace, thread several lengths of waxed string with groups of beads, using knots for spacers. At regular intervals add short lengths of beaded string finished with knots. Gather the main cords together at both ends in bead tips and finish with a spring clasp.

Difficulty level: easy

Designer: Cristina Rosà

Pink organza and bead necklace   *Designer: Roberta Borroni*

Materials:

1.2mm waxed string
Pink beads of various shapes and sizes
Bead tips and spring clasp

Tools:

Flat nose pliers
Scissors

Necklaces with coloured fruits

Thread the beads one at a time on to the black nylon thread by passing the thread twice through each hole and so fixing each bead in position. Make up 4 nylon threads in this way then secure them in the bead tips. Close the necklace with a spring clasp and chain.

Difficulty level: medium   Designer: Maria di Spirito

Materials:

0.35mm black nylon thread
Fruit-shaped beads
Bead tips
Spring clasp and chain

Tools:

Flat nose pliers
Round nose pliers
Scissors

Antique chain necklace with glass beads and droplets

Prepare various beads and glass droplets by passing headpins through each one. Form loops with the exit ends of the pins and attach these to a larger ring. Attach the rings to the chain along with other beads. Attach a ring pendant to the centre of the chain then complete the necklace by alternating chain links with glass beads up to the clasp.

Difficulty level: medium

Designer: Maria di Spirito

Materials:

Antique copper chain
Glass beads, droplets and rings
Little rings and headpins
Spring clasp and chain

Tools:

Flat nose pliers
Round nose pliers
Wire cutters

21

Amber and sapphire ring choker

Make a choker by alternating beads with rings. Close with a spring catch and chain. Attach a droplet bead to each ring. Between each ring use 2 beads to attach another ring and a droplet bead.

Difficulty level: *medium*

Designer: Maria di Spirito

Materials:

Antique copper chain
Glass beads and droplets
Little rings and pins
Spring clasp and chain

Tools:

Flat nose pliers
Round nose pliers
Wire cutters

23

Ruby ring choker

Make up in the same way as the Amber and sapphire ring choker (see page 22).

Difficulty level: medium

Designer: Maria di Spirito

Materials:

Antique copper chain
Glass beads and droplets
Little rings and pins
Spring clasp and chain

Tools:

Flat nose pliers
Round nose pliers
Wire cutters

Black and white chains

Stick a pin through each pearl or crystal, form a loop at the end of the pin and fix to a link in the necklace. Mount 4 or 5 little crystals in a variety of colours and sizes to each of the chain's links. Secure with a spring clasp.

Difficulty level: *medium*

Designer: Maria di Spirito

Materials:

Black and silver-plated chains
Black and silver-plated headpins
Tubular pendant holder
4mm and 10mm rose-cut crystals
6mm imitation pearls
Spring clasps

Tools:

Flat nose pliers
Round nose pliers

Spring floral choker

Cover 5 strands of 0.8mm metal wire with green tubular satin ribbon. Wrap the green ribbon with 0.40mm copper wire whilst at the same time adding small groups of flowers, leaves and beads. Secure the wire-wrapped ribbons to a length of wire threaded with beads at both ends. Close with a spring clasp.

Difficulty level: complex

Designer: Christine Pizzuto

Materials:

0.8mm and 0.4mm copper wire
Green tubular satin ribbon
Glass leaves in green, red and topaz
Red, orange and topaz metallic beads
Spring clasp and chain

Tools:

Wire cutters
Flat nose pliers
Round nose pliers
Scissors

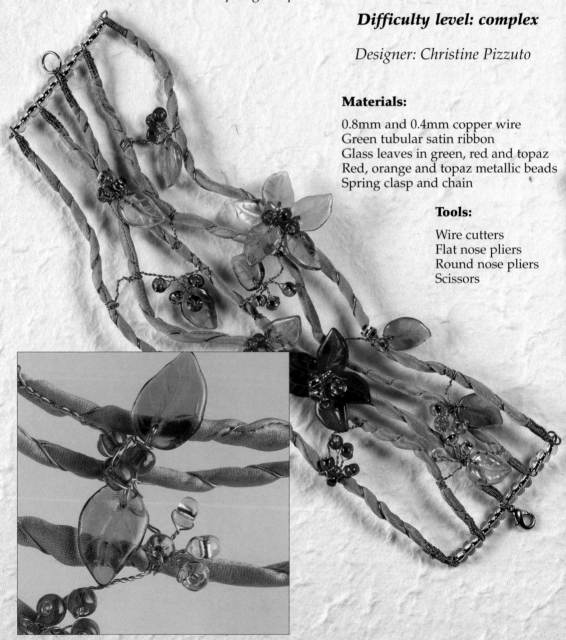

Crocheted necklace with red crystals

Crochet a rope from the 'Fantasy' yarn, inserting the crystals one by one in alternate colours. Join 9 strings of varying lengths in the bead tips and close with a spring clasp.

Difficulty level: easy

Designer: Annarita Aloni

Materials:

0.8mm red 'Fantasy' yarn
10mm rose-cut crystals
Bead tips
Spring clasp

Tools:

Crochet hook
Flat nose pliers
Round nose pliers

Venetian glass flower bead necklace

Make up a group of 10 lengths of waxed cord in matching tones and create 8 groups of beads with knots to space the groups apart. Tie 3 extra lengths of cord to each knot, thread on a bead and secure with a knot. Finish with a buttonhole fastening.

Difficulty level: medium   Designer: Maria di Spirito

Materials:

1mm waxed cord
Venetian glass flower beads
8mm and 10mm rose-cut
crystal beads
Imitation pearls

Tools:

Scissors

33

Necklace in bronze

To make the bead and crystal necklace, cut 6 lengths of nylon coated steel wire and curl it like a ribbon. Thread on bronze seed beads alternating with topaz crystals and glass beads. Secure the strands in a bead tip and decorate with a cover made up of little crystal beads.

Difficulty level: medium

Designer: Maria di Spirito

Materials:

Bronze coloured seed beads
4mm topaz rose-cut crystal beads
Red and topaz glass beads in various sizes
0.20mm nylon thread
0.45mm bronze coloured nylon coated steel wire
Bead tips, little rings and spring clasp

Tools:

Scissors
Flat nose pliers

Bead clusters

Thread several lengths of nylon with green or pink glass beads of alternating sizes. Use a crochet hook to intertwine the nylon thread, whilst inserting the beads one by one. Join the threads together in the clamshell bead tips and close with a spring clasp.

Difficulty level: easy　　　　　　　　*Designer: Maria di Spirito*

Materials:

0.30mm nylon thread
Various styles and sizes of glass beads
Clamshell bead tips
Spring clasp

Tools:

Scissors
Crochet hook

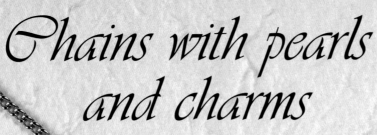

Chains with pearls and charms

Push a pin through each pearl and crystal or attach a ring to a charm, and fix to a link in the chain. Attach 4 or 5 different decorations to each link. Finish with a length of chain with 2 rings, one on each side, and a bar clasp.

Difficulty level: medium

Designer: Maria di Spirito

Materials:

Silver-plated fine and medium chains
Silver-plated headpins and rings
6mm rose-cut crystals
8mm and 12mm artificial pearls
Charms
Ring and bar clasps

Tools:

Flat nose pliers
Round nose pliers
Wire cutters

Choker with cluster pendant

Create a cluster made of wire and beads of the same colour but different shapes. Thread the necklace by alternating small beads with larger beads and pendants. Attach the cluster pendant to the centre.

Difficulty level: medium

Designer: Maria di Spirito

Materials:

Clamshell bead tips and spring clasp
0.55mm gold metal wire
0.35mm nylon coated wire
Round and other shapes of red and white beads

Tools:

Wire cutters
Flat nose pliers

41

Floral red choker

Create 5 clusters of red leaves, then assemble the necklace in the same way as the Choker with cluster pendant (see page 40). Hook the clusters to the necklace at intervals, alternating with the crystal beads.

Difficulty level: *medium*

Designer: Maria di Spirito

Materials:

0.55mm gold metal wire
0.35mm nylon-coated wire
Small leaves in various colours
6mm rose-cut crystals
Clamshell bead tips and spring clasp

Tools:

Wire cutters
Flat nose pliers

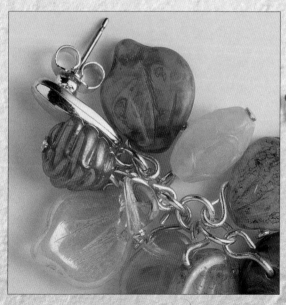

43

Memory wire choker with pendants

Prepare various pendants made up of glass beads mounted on headpins and small rings. Alternate the pendants with crystals and beads on a steel memory wire choker. Thread the sides with beads only and close with a spring clasp.

Difficulty level: medium

Designer: Maria di Spirito

Materials:

6mm smoked topaz
rose-cut crystals
Topaz beads in various shapes
and sizes
0.20mm nylon thread
Roll of memory wire for necklaces
Headpins
Little rings and spring clasp

Tools:

Wire cutters
Round nose pliers

Choker with three roses

Make up 3 roses with nylon thread using 7 central beads and 6 lateral leaves. Mount the three roses on 2 steel wires threaded with rose-cut crystals and imitation pearls. Finish with clamshell bead tips and a spring clasp.

Difficulty level: medium

Designer: Maria di Spirito

Materials:

0.25mm nylon thread
0.45mm nylon coated steel wire
4mm and 6mm rose-cut crystals
3mm and 6mm imitation pearls
Coloured glass leaves
Coloured seed beads
Clamshell bead tips
Spring clasps and chains

Tools:

Flat nose pliers
Scissors

47

Fringed circular pendant

Thread a circle of memory wire with beads, and then close the circle. Embellish the inside of the circle with a variety of beads. Attach 4 beaded pendants to the bottom of the circle and hang the circle on a necklace made up of rose-cut crystal beads.

Difficulty level: medium

Designer: Maria di Spirito

Materials:

Memory wire
0.45mm nylon-coated wire
0.30mm black copper wire
4mm and 6mm rose-cut crystal beads
Glass beads

Tools:

Flat nose pliers
Round nose pliers
Wire cutters

Sugared almond necklaces

Cut a 15cm (6in) length of fine chain. On it mount a variety of beads that have previously been prepared with headpins and place a large bead at each end. Attach the pendant to a length of coloured beads.

Difficulty level: easy

Designer: Maria di Spirito

Materials:

Fine chain
0.45mm nylon-coated steel wire
Round glass beads and glass beads of various sizes
Headpins

Tools:

Flat nose pliers
Round nose pliers
Wire cutters

White teardrop necklace

Prepare 2 nylon-coated steel wires by threading them with alternating white beads and seed beads. Make a ring of seed beads on which to suspend a large teardrop and thread this onto the necklace.

Difficulty level: easy   Designer: Maria di Spirito

Materials:

0.45mm nylon-coated steel wire
Glass beads in various sizes
Silver seed beads
Two-hole bead tip
Bead tips

Tools:

Flat nose pliers
Round nose pliers
Wire cutters

Satin yarn with transparent coloured beads

Put together approximately 150
strands of polyester satin yarn and tie
knots at regular intervals, alternating them
with large transparent glass beads of the same
colour as the yarn. Finish with a knot.

Difficulty level: easy

Designer: Maria di Spirito

Materials:

Polyester satin yarn
Large transparent coloured beads

Tools:

Scissors

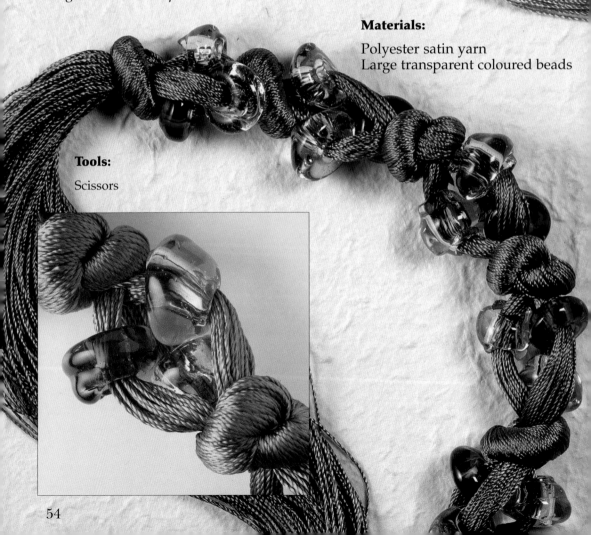

Necklace with lilac dichromatic glass pendant

Wrap the silver wire irregularly around the pendant a few times. As you are doing this, add a few small beads and shells. Thread a length of steel wire with alternating seed beads, shells and pearls then entwine the wire with the waxed cord, and secure with bead tips. Finish with a spring clasp and hang the pendant from the centre.

Difficulty level: medium

Designer: Amarilli Reggiani

Materials:

0.45mm nylon-coated steel wire
1mm lilac waxed cord
0.45mm silver wire
Small shells
Seed beads
Beads
Dichromatic glass pendant

Tools:

Wire cutters
Flat nose pliers
Round nose pliers
Scissors

Coloured glass fusion

Stitch a silk tube and thread through the hole in the glass pendant. Secure the silk necklace in a bead tip and close with a spring clasp and chain.

Difficulty level: easy

Designer: Maria di Spirito

Materials:

Silk fabric
Fused glass pendant
Bead tips
Spring clasp and chain

Tools:

Cutter
Flat nose pliers
Scissors

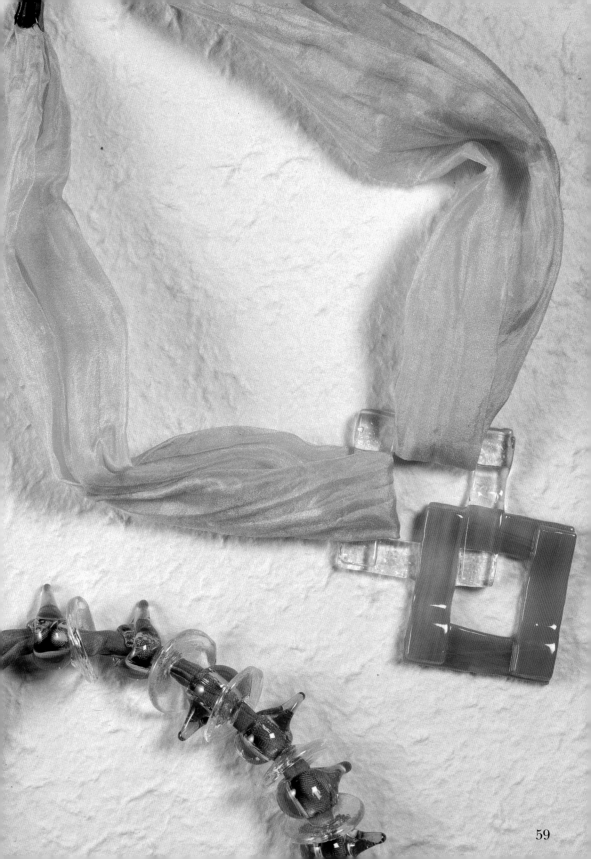

Venetian millefiore choker

Alternate groups of beads, separated by knots, with millefiore, glass beads and metal spacers. Finish with a buttonhole fastener.

Difficulty level: easy

Red choker
Designer: Sabrina Marangoni

Black Necklace
Designer: Roberta Borroni

Materials:

1mm waxed cord
Metal spacers
Glass beads
Millefiore beads

Tools:

Scissors

61

Ethnic necklace with red beads and metal

Thread 6 lengths of yarn with glass beads and metal spacers to form groups separated by knots. Close with a buttonhole fastener.

Difficulty level: easy   *Designer: Maria di Spirito*

Materials:

0.8mm red 'Fantasy' yarn
Metal spacers
Glass beads

Tools:

Scissors

The author is an employee of Fantasy Craft of Milan, which specialises in the production and sale of jewellery supplies. It also offers courses in Venetian bead-making and beading craft.

Readers who would like to see the beads featured in the courses should visit www.fantasycraft.it

The author Maria di Spirito and her colleague Annarita Aloni photographed at Fantasy Craft